WHO IS DONALD TRUMP?

Donald Trump and Hillary Clinton's Race To The White House

MICHAEL BRIXTON

Contents

Who Is Donald Trump?	v
Donald's Introduction: People Just Like Trump!	vii
1. The Day Drumpf went Trump	1
2. Boisterous Beginnings	7
3. The Apprentice President	12
Hillary's Introduction: Thinking the World Of You	18
4. She is Unbeatable	20
5. Bouncing Off the Glass Ceiling	23
6. Likeable Enough and Other Tragedies	27
7. Wiping the Slate Clean	30
Conclusion: The Greatest Challenge	33
The Road Ahead	36
Epilogue	38
8. Hillary's Formative Years	39
9. Hillary as First Lady	43
10. Hillary the Politician	48
11. The Issues and Controversies	53

Who Is Donald Trump?

*Donald Trump and Hillary Clinton's
Race to the White House*

Michael Brixton

Donald's Introduction: People Just Like Trump!

Who is Donald Trump? Like him or hate him. With a surging leading in all of the polls a lot of Americans are asking this question. And if you had asked it 20 years ago the answers may have been pretty vague. Back then if you asked people on the street who Donald Trump was, three main topics of conversation may have come out of their mouth. All centered around a guy with unusual hair, a rich guy with unusual hair, and a rich guy with unusual hair that had just divorced Ivana Trump.

You see back in those days, people only heard about Trump if he some tabloid magazine wanted to do a spoof on him and one of his ex-wives. Anything beyond prenuptial agreements and the *personal* affairs of Trump and his supermodel ex-wives was instant fodder for the media, but when it came to his own endeavors as a truly ingenious business man, the press was silent, they didn't want to hear it, solid stories about Trump's business acumen was not deemed entertaining enough to be newsworthy.

How ironic it is then by the time of the reality show, "The Apprentice" trumps main butter was, well, just being Trump and displaying his incredible business sense to a world that was hungry to better itself. It just goes to show you that no matter how clever the media and the news industry thinks it is, sometimes it is one step behind what the people really want. Most TV moguls at the time of the Apprentice's debut laughed themselves silly at the idea that the American public would waste their prime time hours to watch a seasoned business man like Trump lecture random people about how they can get rich like him. But guess what? They were wrong and the Apprentice and its later incarnation of the "Celebrity Apprentice" went on to become the top-rated show on NBC.

Those in the media that pride themselves in knowing what the people want made a fatal mistake in second guessing the Apprentice, and now that Trump is running for President he's hedging his bets that they are making that same mistake once again. Which certainly seemed to be the case in the opening salvo's of his bid to run in the Republican primaries. When Trump made his announcement initial announcement, the media barely even took him seriously.

As supporters rallied in droves to the Donald all the major news networks claimed it was just a fad, just a passing phase. But once it became clear that the fad had really caught on, many in the media started their own personal campaign to latch on Donald Trump's words and jump onto every little thing that they thought they could use to knock him out of the race.

But even though every other morning news reporters were gleefully reporting supposed, "Controversial Comments" that they hoped to hang over Trump's head like a noose. To their utter amazement, nothing stuck, the "Teflon Don" remained unscathed, and the American people didn't seem to care what the news media said about him. This time around they weren't going to be lead and mind controlled by the signals and cues of the media when they attempted to launch buzzwords and bywords to take Trump down, people just weren't buying it. And to the media and the entire political establishment's complete shock, as Donald Trump himself asserts, "People just like Trump!"

1

The Day Drumpf went Trump

Family trees are amazing pieces of history. I remember when I first saw my own family tree what an eye opening experience it was. It was intriguing to learn of the struggles my weary ancestors had to undergo to immigrate to the United States from Holland over 100 years ago. The narratives of their life stories are long and multi-faceted and many of the realities they faced are stranger than fiction to us. And so is the case with Trump's family history, many things about his family past may be different than you might think they would be, including his name itself.

BECAUSE IN SOME alternate universe somewhere we might be talking about all the latest gossip and intrigue revolving around the candidacy of Donald Drumpf, not Donald Trump. And no, that's not a typo; Trump's ancestral last name is "Drumpf". Because it was the Donald's grandfather Fredric Trump who upon immigrating from Germany in 1885 who permanently changed the family name. For him it was just a matter of expediency, and making the first of many business decisions, he quickly decided it would be best for him to anglicize his name.

SADLY, immigrants were often stigmatized in those days, especially if you had an unusual sounding first name; the push to conform to English was very strong. This being the case, German and Irish immigrants often changed their names to better reflect where they lived. The pressure to conform was just that great. So Trump's grandfather seeking success rather than uniqueness, or cultural identity, gladly switched up his name to one that might better bring in the fortune he so desperately desired.

ALWAYS WANTING to seize upon grandeur and greatness, Grandpa Trump, a savvy business man just like his grandson, wanted to change the name to something that was captivating and yet still easily recognizable to everyone who heard it, and so in a moment of inspiration with his mind shuffling faster than a deck of cards, he pulled out the "Trump" card and Drumpf was no more.

BEFORE THIS RATHER UNCEREMONIOUS dumping of the family name however, the Drumpf family had a long history in their ancestral West German village of Kallstadt. And as it turns out the Trumps are not the only famous family to come out of this village. The Heinz family, of Heinz ketchup fame, also hails from this old Bavarian village. And in yet another ironic twist of fate, bringing things even more full circle; this village also connects one of the most prominent stars of the Democratic Party, John

Kerry, into the picture, through his wife Theresa Heinz Kerry.

AMAZINGLY THIS SLEEPY little German village seems to have had a surprisingly long history of big names and celebrities that have drifted in and out of its vicinity. So much so that the local people have taken to calling the place "Die Brulljesmacker" which in German, literally translates as, "The Show Off's". Well, that's absolutely fantastic. I can hear Carli Fiorni now, "Oh Donald give it a rest already! You are such a Brulljesmacker!" Well, maybe not quite! But you get the point, and even the Donald must be proud of a town that is just as larger than life than he is.

When Trumps Grandfather first arrived in New York he was only 16, but he worked hard and began his career as of all things as an "apprentice" to a barber at a local barber shop. There he worked the simple life of many immigrants, doing menial labor, just cutting hair and trimming beards. And in those hard times it was steady work that many would have been happy to have, but being a visionary in a long line of visionaries, Fredric Trump always saw more.

SO AFTER SO MANY days of cutting and sweeping up other people's hair, he decided he had enough of it, and needed something better. And then without another word, he picked up everything and headed out west to Seattle to check out the flourishing Gold mining culture that was prevalent there at the time. It was here that Donald's grandfather became quite an entrepreneur, eventually running a successful restaurant on the rougher side of town where the guns out numbered the people. Always living dangerously he set up shop where others had feared to tread, and as a result it paid him back tremendously, when his lone little restaurant became a Mecca for the thousands of gold miners that passed through the area.

He was doing well, but being the man of opportunity that he was, when he heard of the monumental event of the "Klondike Gold Rush" in 1897", Fredrich Trump dropped everything and ran up to a town that was one of the main focal points of the rush, Bennet, British Columbia and opened up a brand new restaurant he named the "New Arctic Restaurant and Hotel."

AS THE THOUSANDS of prospectors came streaming in, Trump found a goldmine of his own, and quickly monopolized on the business they brought him. It was here that Fredrich Trump learned to navigate an underworld with a whole host of interesting characters. And these characters who always paid their weight in gold, no questions asked, came to have much influence on Grandpa Trump's club. According to some reports, the place quickly became a counter cultural underworld.

A LITERAL DEN OF THIEVES, gamblers and hustlers nestled right in the middle of the gold rush. According to one report from the Yukon Sun Newspaper, a stampeder from the time commented that, "For single men the Arctic has excellent accommodations as the best restaurant in Bennet, but I would not advise respectable women to go there to sleep as they are liable to hear that which would be repugnant to their feelings and uttered too by the depraved of their own sex."

. . .

SO, if we believe the commentary from one visitor from the time, it was a great business, with some great food and service, but also one that served the underworld of the gold rush. But regardless of the opinion's about certain clientele, old grandpa Trump's business was booming and by 1897 he was open practically 24 hours and the enterprising Trump was dishing out about 3000 meals a day to the rough and tumble of the Gold Rush, but when those who were once pouring in began to decline in numbers, the ever eager Trump began to look elsewhere. The slowing down of his clientele was also compounded with the problems of his then business partner Ernest Levin, who was an incurable alcoholic, drinking up most of his wages in the bottle.

FACED with such depressing circumstances Fredrich Trump finally decided he had had enough and cashed in his business, making a huge profit in the process. He was so well off in fact; he decided to go back to Germany, taking his new found wealth and finance back to the homeland with him. But rather than investing all that money back into the country off his birth, fate had different plans for Fredrich and his future Trump family. Because every single time he tried to repatriate himself back to his country he was rejected at every turn.

GERMAN OFFICIALS DENIED him access to the land of his birth for a variety of reasons. They accused him of leaving the country to evade taxes. Another reason for the denial was that he had shirked military service in the German army. And then amazingly the number one reason they cited for his denial was that he didn't ask them for proper permission in the first place. This bizarre legal wrangling went on and on. But it was due to these accusations that Fredrich Drumpf was ultimately denied repatriation back to his own country and forced to head back to the United States.

HE HAD RATHER IRONICALLY, somehow been deemed an "illegal immigrant" in his own country, which is even more ironic in light of some of his grandson's views on modern day immigration. His return home wasn't a complete loss though, because although being repatriated back to Germany had eluded him, love had not. Because it was during this trip back that Trump literally married the "girl next door". Because it was during all of his legal struggles back in Germany that he became reacquainted with Elizabeth Christ an old friend from the neighborhood that he grew up in.

IT WAS this lovely young lady that would become the matriarch of the future Trump family. And it was her first born son Fred Trump Jr., who became the first rising star of the now fully Americanized Trump family dynasty. Born in 1905, by the time of his death in 1999 he had left his son Donald Trump with millions of dollars worth of real-estate value and incalculable wealth in business real politics. A dynasty that began with a downtrodden and down on his luck immigrant, buoyed by his son a real estate magnate and entrepreneurial genius, and then solidified into world wide fame by the ever boisterous grandson who was much more than an apprentice. They really did pull a trump card out of the deck on the day that Drumpf went Trump.

2

Boisterous Beginnings

Donald J. Trump was born on June 14th 1946, in Queens, New York. Being one among five children, even though he was born into a house of means, the competition was fierce, and Donald found himself fighting for everything he could get, whether it was money, resources, or extra attention from his mom and dad. It was a tough tenacity that his father Fred Jr. took note of early on, he was in fact, so impressed by what he viewed as the Donald's innate, "scrappiness" that he really felt that this was a stand out feature that could propel his son to success some day.

But in the meantime the young Trump had to get through grade school. Even though his toughness would serve him well later in life, the sixth grade wasn't the board room, and his over the top aggressive behavior often got the young Trump in trouble. His energy level was through the roof and the dower old private Kew-Forest School literally just couldn't contain his enthusiasm.

His father realizing that Donald needed a good outlet for his passion decided it would be best to ship off his son to military school at the tender age of 13. Usually when you hear stories like this, they don't end well and the son or daughter sent off to boarding school or the military academy are extremely bitter with their parents for putting them in such a predicament. This was not the case with Donald Trump, he absolutely loved it there, and just as his dad had imagined his scrappiness and fierceness of spirit served him well in that environment. Trump contends to this day that going to military school was the best thing that had ever happened to him, teaching him to be organized and channel his energies in a product and positive way.

It was a gamble that Fred Trump Jr. had made, betting on the prospect he would do well in a rigidly structured environment. And fortunately he was right because the New York Military academy could be a rough place and not everyone that was sent there was able to make it through to the end. But not Donald, the competitive atmosphere served Donald Trump well and it was within the confines of this academy that he forged a hawkish sort of intellect, learning how to bargain to get his way. Performing well both athletically and socially, he was a top notch athlete and student leader. Graduating in 1964, he was already a success story and had managed to seize hold of that attention that he had always struggled for since the day he was born.

Four years later Trump would triumph again by graduating with honors from the prestigious University of Pennsylvania's Wharton School of Finance in 1968. Then with his Bachelor's still fresh in his hand, a vibrant and energetic 22 year old Donald Trump joined his father's company and by 1974 Donald became President of the firm, and renamed it the "Trump Organization". Laying hold of the company that would take the world by storm, here we can see the beginnings of empire beginning to form. Although

Trump was born with certain advantages, once he was in the drivers seat he took things farther than anyone else.

Because once the baton was passed and the reigns of power were handed over from father to son, Trump did not just inherit, he invested and from there Mr. Trump took the business to new heights of success that his father had only dreamed of. For most of the 1980's Donald Trump was like royalty in New York and jumped from one success story to another, which quickly earned him the name of "Mr. Midas" but as the decade wore to a close and Trump's aspirations grew ever larger, his Midas touch began to weaken and fade. And when Donald Trump finally went bankrupt in 1991 the news media went absolutely wild.

He was written off as a failure, a buffoon, and prime example of nepotism gone awry by not just strangers, but sadly it was even those closest to him that began to extend their feet to kick him when he was down. Where did it all go wrong? He went from the "Art of the Deal" to the art of finding the next meal; as his businesses collapsed around him and even the Teflon Don's own personal finances were on the verge of bankruptcy. Just how did all this happen?

It didn't happen all at once but the first major blow to Trump's empire began with the failure of his prized Taj Mahal Casino. This was a building that began with the complete promise of taking the gaming world of Atlantic City casino's by storm. The real estate in the area had been neglected for sometime and Trump had dreams of replacing all the urban blight in the area with his own brand name. The Taj had every reason to do well and it was opened with the greatest of fanfare, but even the 1990 star power of Michael Jackson couldn't keep this business afloat.

Because when it was all said and done, he was suddenly

$9.2 billion dollars in debt. And as Trump himself tells it, he really knew he was in trouble when he saw a beggar on the street and realized that this beggar with absolutely nothing was in fact $9.2 billion dollars wealthier than his own negative 9.2 billion that had just been flushed down the toilet by his failed casino.

Trump's biggest mistake when he invested in the Taj Mahal Casino was that he did so with high interest rate junk bonds, with a shelf life shorter than a piece of pastrami on a hot New Jersey sidewalk. Donald remembers this loss from a business venture laced in high interest junk bonds that was doomed for failure as an important life lesson in resilience. He had to be resilient to survive. In order to avoid total collapse Trump was eventually forced to give up half of his ownership of the casino in order to retain any control over the property at all. His largest creditor in all of this was financial wizard Carl Icahn who held out $400 million in bonds. One of the few people who truly had Trump's back during this crisis, with a save like that, it is really no coincidence that Mr. Icahn will be Trump's pick for Treasury Secretary if he ever gets elected President.

And speaking of financial collapse, bankruptcy and the presidency; in his run for the White House, as much as his bankrupt business ventures of the past have been criticized, in true Trump fashion, the Donald doesn't hide from these dealings, but actually embraces them. He champions the bankruptcies that he has been through as a positive sign which demonstrates that he has the tenacity to lead perhaps the biggest bankruptcy of all; that of the United States economy. Because it is the United States itself that Mr. Trump has continually asserted as being a bankrupt country that better go into default sooner, rather than later, in order to fix it.

So is it just another "art of the deal" to slap on a one-size fits all Chapter 11 on the United States of America? Believe it or not, many experts believe this is exactly what the American economy needs. Because right now the country's debt has skyrocketed in that all too familiar game of an exponentially increasing interest payment being paid by raising the ever increasing "debt ceiling" and then borrowing more money to pay for what has already been borrowed. A vicious cycle that has led many to conclude that a default is just around the corner.

This default, could take on the form of what has been termed a selective default, most likely focusing a default in one of two areas; by either defaulting on the 2.4 trillion that it owes the Federal Reserve or perhaps even more alarming, defaulting with the 1.2 trillion that is owed to China. A partial default is something that Trump has been alluding to for quite some time. It was back in the fiscal crisis of 2011 that Trump voiced a challenge to the Republicans to not back down from their talks until they "got what they wanted". And in the process Trump encouraged the Republicans to use the so-called "nuclear option" of letting the U.S. officially go into default. What can these extreme measures possibly solve? Is breaking it the only way of fixing it? Would Donald Trump really tell the United States Government, "You're fired?"

3

The Apprentice President

When the business based reality show, "The Apprentice" began back in 2004 who knew that it would make Donald Trump such a star? The man that so often was depicted as a dopey, cartoonish, buffoon of a character from the New York world of privilege, suddenly against all odds, became "cool".

Through the power of television, public perception of the Donald changed dramatically and after seeing his wheeling and dealing charisma on their evening television night after night, America looked past the tabloids and media attacks and decided they saw something that they very much liked, even admired in Donald J. Trump. Something they liked so much, in fact, that the Donald was quite surprised by all the adulation himself, and has since then remarked over how being the star of the "hottest" show on TV definitely has its perks.

And if we look at the pre-Apprentice Trump and the post-Apprentice Trump, the facts tend to weigh this out. Because just to put things into perspective, right before the Apprentice came out Donald Trump was just your average every day billionaire (as average as that is), and now he is a celebrity in his own right! Even earning a star on the Hollywood walk of fame! The world has now taken great notice of the Donald and apparently so did the hair police as well, because one of the number one topics revolving around Donald Trump is his hair!

And it was precisely in regard to the mop on top of his head, that he got into his first post apprentice beef with Joy Behar when she criticized him and accused him of wearing a hair piece! In retaliation Trump is quoted as calling her, "A woman with no talent and a terrible accent, who again attacked my hair". These are the kind of brutal take down maneuvers that we have come to expect from Trump, and this "take no crap" kind of demeanor is what many have grown to know and love.

Others however see a much more disturbing picture beginning to emerge, and liken his antics to that of a bully, and one that has very uniquely targeted women. Making some wonder if Donald Trump has a deep seated bias against women. But whatever it is, it can't really be said that Trump works to hold women back. This is especially evident when you take into account the fact that the most successful candidates on his reality show, more often than not were female. But although this data makes may make Donald Trump seem like a rather benign and equality of the sexes supporting fellow.

The notion is severely side tracked however when you couple this "progress" with Trump's own assertion that his female apprentice's success was due in large part to their sex appeal. In his book "How to Get Rich" he offhandedly remarks, "All the women on the Apprentice flirted with me —consciously or unconsciously. That's to be expected. A sexual dynamic is always present between people, unless you are asexual." These are the classic Donald Trump over the top and absurdly blunt statements that make some people life and others cry.

But one thing Donald Trump has definitely never been one to deny, is his own sexual dynamics, the man who claims to "cherish" women even famously bought up the Miss Universe Organization in 1996. To be exact, Trump bought half of the rights to Miss Universe, and allowed CBS to control the other half. It was through the control of this major televised venue broadcast over CBS that Donald Trump's first major fires into the world of television had begun.

In the beginnings of his dealings with CBS trump was a direct partner and became fascinated with how the business of television worked. Amazingly, Trump turned out to be a great TV promoter, and garnered more interest and attention for the pageant than it had had in many years. In 2002 he had the show doing better than ever, ranking at number seven for the week and number one by demographic. Trump the real estate turned TV mogul was doing very well for himself and after the pageant outdid NBC's coverage of the NBA play offs, trump gained an even more persistent fan base, as NBC executives came scrambling to his door to offer him a better deal.

Yes, it seems that after their ratings had taken a hit from Trumps ingenious marketing of Miss Universe, NBC was singing a tune of, "If you can't beat em', join em." with this major network seeking to take CBS's place as Trump's partner. It seems that even before the Apprentice, NBC wanted *to be* Trump's apprentice!

After NBC made several ovations his way, Trump made up his mind and bought out the rest of Miss Universe from CBS (They didn't have a chance!) and then struck his new TV deal with NBC. And Trump came ready with a package of new ideas that would send a simple beauty pageant competition like Miss Universe into a realm of cross marketing no one had ever dream, as Trump laid out ideas for combined plots and themes, such as, among other things, his "Miss Universe Fear Factor".

Do you remember that show? Fear Factor? It was a popular stunts show in the early 2000's that put average every day people into fearful situations such as eating bugs or walking through fire. Trump's basic premise then was, ok, let's do the fear factor thing, except this time with super models! It may seem like a goofy and simplistic combination, but really it shows Trump's genius insight, he knows what makes a hit, and knows how to add more hit material (like supermodels) to make it an even greater hit.

It is this bizarre simplicity that is often what is so ingenious about Trump, instead of making things harder or more complicated than they should be Trump finds what he wants and goes right after it. His acquisition of Miss Universe is a major embodiment of that mentality, when asked once in an interview why he would waste his time handling this pageant he said very bluntly, "I love beautiful women and I'm also a businessman, so it seemed like a good idea, which it has turned out to be." It turned out to be an excellent idea for him and it is his very blunt wheeling's and dealings that has made him a very successful man. And it was in this prime position that Donald just happened upon Mark Burnett the creator of Survivor.

The live finale of the series was planned to be broadcast out of a section of Central Park that Mr. Trump just happened to own, so they had to approach him for permission to begin shooting the show, but they ended up approaching him with much more. As it turns out Mark Burnett is a huge fan of Donald Trump and when he introduced himself to the Donald the fireworks went off, and Burnett instantly launched into new plans for a reality show starring none other than Donald Trump.

Being the businessman that he is, Trump did not jump into this TV role without forethought, but after mulling it over he could definitely see the potential. And when Mark Burnett rattled off to Trump that filming would only require 3 hours a week, the deal was sealed and led Trump on an odyssey for one of the most popular reality TV shows out there.

And now that he has become a candidate for President of the United States, having the role of reality TV star has had its champions as well as its critics. It was Wisconsin Governor Scott Walker who during a heated primary debate quipped, "Mr. Trump, we don't need an apprentice in the White house." A nice play on words from his opponents, but one that drives home a point, although Trump is successful in the boardroom, can he go from apprentice to President?

Conclusion: You've Been Trumped

I was actually out of the country when Donald Trump announced his candidacy for President in the summer of 2015. I remember coming back to the United States in late July and feeling like the whole world must have turned upside down. When I was waiting at the airport in DC to transfer my flight, Trump was plastered across every television I the airport. Did I just wake up in the twilight zone? What the hell just happened?

Don't get me wrong I always liked Donald Trump and appreciated his unique (to say it lightly) personality. But I never really imagined him as a president; I'm not saying it isn't possible, because I fully believe it is. But I never imagined that the man would actually run. I had heard people reference him as a political contender years ago, especially in 2012, but I never thought Trump took it that seriously.

Who Is Donald Trump?

As the whole world may have noticed though, Trump seems to be taking his 2016 candidacy very seriously. And even though he is forced to sign pledges in his own party, he has an energy (Sorry Jeb Bush!) that his opponents can not match

But can he really win? I don't see why not. As surprised as some are that a celebrity/business man non-politician can take on the establishment as well as he does, this is nothing new. There have always been those outsider, shake-up candidates in politics. And although they make major party platforms like Democrats and Republicans extremely nervous, I believe that these mavericks (Yes, John McCain!) have their purpose in revolutionizing the field. And as befuddled as some of the "established" crowd are, it just goes to show you how you can liven up a game, with just a little pull of the trump card.

Hillary's Introduction: Thinking the World Of You

Most Americans think they know Hillary Clinton pretty well, after all, a whole generation of young people practically grew up with either a Clinton in political office, or a Clinton who was otherwise attempting to obtain it. Hillary's resume is a long one, she was a high powered attorney as a young woman, and by her 30's was riding it out as first lady of Arkansas with her husband, then Governor, Bill Clinton.

SHE WOULD THEN FOLLOW her husband to the white house for two successful terms. And then upon her husband's exit from world politics, she would again thrust herself onto the world stage getting elected to the Senate in New York. Being Senator of New York was a great achievement in itself, but for many who placed their hopes for the first female president firmly on Hillary Clinton's shoulders, this Senate Seat was just an obvious stepping stone for the true prize; that of President of the United States of America.

Who Is Donald Trump?

. . .

SO SHE RAN IN 2008, and through the blood, sweat, and tears of determination she tried her best, and then to everyone, most especially her own, disbelief, she failed, and it was Barack Obama, not Hillary Clinton that became the next leader of the free world. For someone who had been on a roll of non stop achievement over the past 30 years, it was incredible to finally experience failure.

COMING in second was never something Hillary took lightly, and even after she was appointed Secretary of State in the Obama Administration, another run was never far off the table. So here we are in 2016 and Hillary Clinton is setting her sights to take another shot at what she so famously described as the "final glass ceiling". And whatever your personal sentiment is toward her, you have to respect her sheer tenacity and will when it comes to breaking down barriers.

ACCORDING to Bill Clinton she is "the smartest" person he knows. Even though the two have had more than their fair share of difficulties, with statements like that, it is clear that he thinks the world of his accomplished wife. What Bill Clinton wants now more than anything though, is the reverse of that affection, and have the whole world think of his wife as she achieves not only her dreams but theirs as well.

4

She is Unbeatable

By many accounts Hillary's political ambition is not something that was spawned in Washington DC. It didn't come about as a result of her husband's tenure as President, or even the decade the two spent together in the Governor's mansion in Arkansas. No, for many who had witnessed it, they say that the rising star of Hillary's future Presidency took off in the spring of 1969 at Wellesley College.

In the hallowed halls of Wellesley there was not anything that seemed so readily special about Hillary at first glance. She was just an undergraduate student like everyone else, anticipating her Bachelor's after four long years of work, but her college President Ruth Adams saw more, and breaking with precedent granted Hillary the right to speak at commencement. It was a spur of the moment kind of decision, but when Hillary spoke to that crowd on May 31st, 1969 it was electrifying. It was one of those rare moments where one speaker can somehow connect to hundreds of spectators, as if they are all talking one on one, it was an amazing sight to see. In her speech

Hillary encouraged, civil disobedience, she encouraged protest, and she encouraged dissent.

It was these roots of social discord that many conservatives point to in order to brand Hillary Clinton as a radical. When you paint with such a wide paint brush however, you have to be careful, because you just might find that you have painted yourself in a corner. The truth is, Hilary was no more radical than most 22 year olds were in 1969. The end of the 60's was an extremely volatile and tumultuous time in our nation's history. Sure Hillary went to a few protests, but who didn't? It was the 60's for crying out loud! Back then when young people found an excuse to pal around in public with each other, it often took on the form of some kind of sit in or civic protest, it was just as much a social club as it was meaningful social action.

But no matter what anyone's reasoning was, when it came to the call for public service, Hillary was a firm believer in the cause. When she left Wellesley to begin her instruction at Yale Law School she was a vocal member of the "Yale Review of Law and Social Action". It was here that she first began to put together social legislation to help some of the most vulnerable and desperate of society. This was the mission statement of her law review in the 1970's and in many ways it became the mission statement of her entire life, as she has always viewed herself as the champion of the downtrodden.

And during her Yale Law days it was the sad lot of disadvantaged children that she fought the hardest to improve. Not only did she have empathy for the plight of strangers. Because when Clinton looked at some of these struggling children she couldn't help but think of the heartbreaking story of her mother's own upbringing. Because Dorothy's mom, Dorothy Rodham had it about as bad as any young person could.

Dorothy was the daughter of two very troubled parents. The home situation was volatile and often violent. As rare as it is, Hillary's father was a battered spouse, and was often on the receiving end of severe beatings from his wife. When men are abused by women it usually goes unreported and undocumented, but the abuse that Dorothy's father suffered is surprisingly well recorded with even his own sister in law testifying against her own flesh and blood sister saying that she, "had a violent temper and flew at him in a rage, and would fight him."

The court actually took these charges very seriously, so seriously in fact that Dorothy's mom was immediately declared unfit to be a mother as a consequence. This left only the father for her care and support, but he was not psychologically or financial able to take care of his daughter so he had her shipped off to her grandparents in Chicago. Adjusting to life in Chicago was hard for Dorothy and the fact that her grandparents didn't want her there certainly didn't help.

Tragically, according to Hillary's mother, Dorothy was viewed as nothing more than an unnecessary burden that was foisted upon them by the courts and her father. These toxic sentiments put the young Dorothy in a horrible place emotionally that no one should have to go through. Hearing such sad testimony from her mother's childhood is what led Hillary to champion children's rights so passionately later on in life. Hearing this tale of how a botched ruling from the courts landed her mother in a house full of misery led her to fight for children's rights in the determination of their own custody.

This was cutting edge litigation back in the 1970's and Hillary was at the head of it. She fought to give children a voice where they were usually voiceless. This theme was the centerpiece of "Children of the Law: a major article that Hillary wrote for the Harvard Educational Review. This article relates testimony and incidents of children, like her mother, who found themselves placed in rather precarious positions by the courts who had sworn to protect them.

The article then goes on to stress that sometimes the voice of the child needs to be heard and competency hearings should be conducted to ascertain whether or not a child is able to competently decide what home they should go to. Such competency hearings may be fairly common today, but back in the 1970's they were rare, and Hillary was on the cutting edge of it. Being the visionary that she is, Hillary seems to have a great knack for seeing just a little bit further than everyone else.

And this was a foresight that was widely noted and appreciated for the first time when she was first lady of Arkansas. Even though the local newspapers liked to joke that her great vision came from the wide rimmed glasses she always wore during Bill Clinton's tenure as Governor, the more serious minded around here knew that this mental tenacity came from somewhere else entirely. Because those that know Hillary know that he best ideas come to her when she is in deep thought, they seem to just get pulled out from somewhere deep in her being. It seems that when Hillary Clinton can tune the world out and tune herself in, she is unbeatable.

5

Bouncing Off the Glass Ceiling

In the year 1992, Bill and Hillary Clinton were flying all over the country campaigning their hearts out for the chance to be President and first lady of the United States. And what was I doing? I was probably in the corner somewhere playing with Lego's! But you have to cut me some slack since I was only about 9 years old at the time. Even so, I remember looking up from my pile of Lego's to see the fascinating visage of this political power couple beamed onto my parent's TV set and realizing that there was something very interesting about this pair.

BILL CLINTON HAD a charm and charisma that could leap right out of the TV set at you and Hillary seemed like a well oiled analytical machine, perfectly constructed, perfectly maintained, and able to answer any and all of life's questions that were thrown her way. All that is, except for one, because of all things, it was when that jolly ever to peppy reporter half jokingly asked her, "And Mrs. Clinton…when are you going to run for President?" That Hillary froze in her tracks.

HER OWN HUSBAND always joked about it and even alluded to a potential co-presidency by referring to their husband and wife partnership as "Two for the Price of One". What about Hillary's own ambition to be the leader of the free world? They were undeniably there, but she always put them on the back burner with service to her husband and his endeavors first and foremost on her mind. The desire for her own administration never waned however, and as soon as her husband's term was over, she was vying for the Senator seat of New York.

THIS MEANT that the Clinton base was very much split into two camps during the 2000 election cycle; those that put forth all of their energy into the Gore presidential campaign of that year and those that raised funds for Hillary's Senate race. It may not seem like a big deal at first, they are both running two separate tickets for two separate positions, without much interaction. But the campaign funds are another story, and they most certainly do interact.

IN FACT STAFF members of the Gore presidential campaign were so upset by the interference that Hillary's bid in the Senate had caused, they accused Hillary of directly sucking into their purse strings, and absorbing political donations that otherwise would have went directly to Al Gore. The Gore campaign had their suspicions for a while, but couldn't quite place where the money drain was coming from.

BUT WHEN HILLARY showed up at a fundraiser that was supposed to be for Gore, she was supposed to be there to support him, but instead stormed the stage and after addressing the audience reminded them to vote Hillary for the Senate. It was this self-centered campaign style that Mr. Gore could do without. What Gore could also do without was the interference by Hillary's husband Bill Clinton. Although they were in the same political party, Bill Clinton didn't seem particularly thrilled with the candidacy of his successor Al Gore and instead of throwing his weight behind Gore he put all of his energy into Hillary Clinton's campaign for the New York senate.

AND LIKE A FORCE OF GRAVITY, pulling political fortunes his way, Mr. Gore's star inevitably receded while Hillary's rose to new heights. Gore famously lost in the tight race of 2000, while Hillary won her Senate seat by a large 55 percent margin, knocking her opponent Rick Lazio right out of the water. This is the point that Hillary really became a major power player n the Democratic Party. While Mr. Gore's dreams were dashed, Hillary's were realized and even though she would later fail to win the Presidency in 2008, the rising star of Hillary Clinton has yet to wane. It may have bounced off a glass ceiling here and there, but in time it will rise again.

6

Likeable Enough and Other Tragedies

If overconfidence isn't Hillary Clinton's greatest weakness, then maybe this trait could be shifted a bit and it could be said that the overconfidence of those *around* her are *her* greatest weakness. Because her entire campaign staff during much of the duration of the 2008 campaign had a mindset like the battle was already won during most of the campaign, and viewing their candidate as a shoe in, they advised her accordingly. Many crucial opportunities were missed in the process. In Iowa for example, the place where most Presidential candidates have to go to solidify their lead, Hillary was mainly absent and when she did visit the state she did so more as a relaxed lecturer and guest speaker than as a dynamic and energized Presidential candidate. And the reactions of Iowans reflected this disconnect.

IT WAS the Iowan disconnect that grew into a complete dislike of the whole Hillary Clinton persona. In her campaign strategy to appear to be above the fray, Hillary

Clinton floated herself so far above it, she almost missed it entirely. And when her campaign staff finally pulled their heads out of the clouds (and other not nice places) the race for the White House was almost over.

IN THE WORLD OF POLITICS, if you miss Iowa, you miss everything, because Iowa represents Middle America and the average voter. It was her lack of personal attention and vigor that caused Iowans to distance themselves from Hillary and embrace Obama. As one local constituent put it, "I had waited a long time to make up my mind and when I decided to support Obama, I had not received a call from the Hillary group and I never attended any of Clinton's functions."

THE AVERAGE VOTER in Iowa felt neglected by Hillary while, Edwards and Obama showered them with attention. Apparently the Clinton campaign staff felt that they were above having to be so proactive in Iowa even though local advisors repeatedly informed them that a much more personal touch was needed. The Clinton team didn't realize this though until it was far too late, and their efforts of damage control only made matters worse and as a result that glass ceiling that Hillary Clinton has often spoke of seemed higher and higher.

IN FULL PANIC mode the Clinton machine desperately scrambled to revamp Hillary's image and sent her out to numerous town hall meetings that allowed her to speak with crowds of various size on the spot. Here she answered questions on a wide area of topics but the most important to her audience were always, the economy, military spending, and military conflict.

SHE INVARIABLY HANDLED ALL of these questions extremely well, but there was one question that would really get her thinking and it had nothing at all to do with health or economy. It was the so called question of likeability. The whole room paused in silence when a man asked, "What can you say to the voters of New Hampshire on this stage tonight who see a resume and like it, but are hesitating on the likeability issue, where they seem to like Barack Obama more?

THIS WAS the sad situation that Hillary Clinton was facing, she had tried hard all of her life, she made the grades, she graduated from prestigious schools, she had a long resume of unique experience's and roles she could speak of, but the message they were sending in Iowa was a simple almost childish kind of "nah na boo boo we don't like you". The so-called likeability factor had been touted for quite some time during the campaign as political pundits and spectators pondered over if Hillary was likeable enough to be President.

THERE WAS EVEN a famous quip from Obama on the subject to where when the subject came up, when Obama rather condescendingly declared "You're likeable enough Hillary". As insulting as all this was, at that point in time, she just took it all in stride. Hillary Clinton has learned very well over the years to remain detached and not to take things personal. This is why that rare moment of the moderator managing to hit home with some of her emotions stands out so much. Because once we are able to cut away some of her well earned layers of steel, we can begin to see a much more vulnerable and real Hillary Clinton, and one that even to the surprise of her opponents, is very much likeable.

7

Wiping the Slate Clean

It's not easy being Secretary of State. This could be one of the biggest understatements in the world. In the American system it is the Secretary of State that gets handed off to some of the world's most challenging situations and made to face off against some of the most complicated of international actors. But even while the demands and challenges of the job may be great, the authority given to a Secretary of State to mitigate these difficulties is not. When it comes to real world ability to exert their will, at best, the Secretary of state can be seen as a top level advisor who travels abroad.

AND AT WORST is nothing more than a goodwill ambassador who is soundly criticized and attacked by those that disagree with us or wish us ill. Sadly this is exactly the kind of hyped up punching bag that Hillary Clinton had become during much of the so-called "Arab Spring" when dictators fell and revolutionaries and militants scrambled for power. During this uprising Hillary took most of the blame for Obama's policies, as a whole country vented their rage and disappointment with their own failed social revolution. In their disgust and frustration they certainly did make Hillary Clinton the convenient scapegoat, but what about being powerless?

I COULDN'T IMAGINE A MUCH MORE powerless feeling she could have felt than when the media reports came in on September 11th, 2012 that Christopher Stevens an ambassador she had placed in a consulate in Benghazi Libya, along with three other Americans went up in the smoke of a hateful terrorist attack. At first Hillary seemed as surprised as everyone else, and initially toed the line right along with Susan Rice's assertion that the attack was a spontaneous outburst of anger over a YouTube video.

IT WAS ONLY when the Senate Intelligence report came out afterwards that it was finally made clear that this horrible act of hatred and violence had nothing at all to do with a YouTube video. But was a much larger coordinated attack, and one that the CIA had foreseen ahead of time and actually warned the State Department of its possibility as a threat, suggesting that they increase their security. For whatever reason though these recommendations appear to have fallen on deaf ears.

AS SECRETARY of state appointing and overseeing ambassadors like Chris Stevens was a part of Hillary's job description. Since the secretary of state is essentially the top ambassador of the United States, all of the worlds far flung representatives are essentially under her charge. And that being said, Hillary has taken great strides to claim responsibility what has happened under her watch. She even outlined proactive measures that her leadership over the State Department had taken to make sure that a tragedy of this magnitude would never happen again.

BUT IS that enough to convince the American public? Especially one that is so agitated and ready to take down politicians in a heated election season? New rivals from the Democratic Party like Bernie Sanders have leapt upon these perceived deficiencies in trust, demanding just what she might want to hide in secret e-mails pertaining to the tragic event of Benghazi. And if there are even more embarrassing revelations lurking right around the corner of an e-mail server, it definitely won't bode well for Hillary. Because whether the issue at hand is a server or a severe lack of trust towards her in the American consciousness, the slate just isn't so easily wiped clean.

Conclusion: The Greatest Challenge

Who the hell is Bernie Sanders? If you caught yourself thinking that during Bernie's sudden emergence out of political nowhere in the summer of 2015 you weren't the only one. Before the run up to 2016 began, Bernie Sanders was a little known Senator from the East Coast, that most Americans knew nothing about. In the world of politics this can actually be a good thing. And being branded a political "outsider" like Bernie has been described is an incredible asset. In many ways the less the electorate knows about you the better. That way you are free to shape and mold your image to whatever you think the public wants to see.

For Hillary Clinton, a figure that has been a part of the American lexicon as long as most Americans can remember. This kind of image gymnastics is not quite so easy. She has been hefting some pretty mighty political luggage for years, much longer than any of her competitors, and as much as she may want to leave some of the worst of it at the baggage claim before she gets to the White House, she

Conclusion: The Greatest Challenge

can't. Whether it's offhand comments made when her Husband was governor of Arkansas or the Benghazi tragedy when she was secretary of state, these events are unshakable in the American memory and when thinking of the possibility of Hillary being the President of the United States, they will inevitably come to the surface.

Her immediate recognition has always been her greatest strength and weakness. During 2008 her staffers were so afraid of being drowned out by the image of her husband Bill Clinton, they refused to even mention her last name. I remember seeing all the campaign adds, promotions, and even political buttons that all said simply, "Hillary". They were so afraid of the mental association with Bill that they refused to even let the name "Clinton" come to mind.

But before 2016 most of the baggage that Hillary carried was associated with other people such as her husband. Anything that she had done on her own was mild in comparison. Sure they could pull up some obscure offhand comment form 1992 with Hillary seeming to bash stay at home mothers, talking about not wanting to stay at home baking cookies, but this is really immaterial, and only serves as fodder for late night television hosts. As much as the media tries to push salacious material like that, I'm sure very few stay at home mothers were offended.

In 2016 on the other hand the political burdens she carries is much more serious. Through her tenure as Secretary of State Hillary is integrally linked to the Obama administration. So all of the perceived successes and failures of this President are going to follow her, and not only that, she now has her own administrative record as Secretary of State. Add this to her time as Senator of New York and she

Conclusion: The Greatest Challenge

now has a well documented political history of her own. Combine this with the fact that she has one of the most recognizable names in politics and you have the recipe for drama.

Sure Bernie Sanders wasn't born yesterday, and he has his own record in the Senate, but his name recognition is almost zero for most people, and whatever skeletons he may have in his closet are not likely to stick. For Hillary on the other hand, with her name being one of the most popular key word searches on the planet, there is no way for her to approach this thing from the outside. She has been known to be a very creative problem solver, inventing new strategies and approaches to political life, but it will be the task of reinventing the American opinion of her that will be Hillary Clinton's greatest challenge in 2016.

The Road Ahead

Although we don't know for sure as of this writing (September 2015) who will go head to head during the general election, if the pairing does wind up being Hillary Clinton against Donald Trump it will most definitely turn into quite a sight to see. They both excellent debaters, but have very different styles and approach. Hillary is excellent out throwing counter punches while the Donald when attacked goes on the offensive and outright shuts people down. This match up would more than likely be a knock em dead, drag out fight with the potential to garner even more ratings than the Apprentice. If Donald Trump still has share holdings with NBC he is liable to make a killing whether he actually gets elected or not!

ALL OF THIS attention seeking could backfire and be a source of contention for Donald Trump, but so far it has only worked in his favor. The media has tried to paint him as a narcissist only caring about his own self promotion and glory, and not someone who has the best interest of the country at heart. Although you can't help but think that the Donald's constant third person references to "Trump does this" and "Trump does that" lends credence to this idea, at the same time, you would have to ask, "What presidential candidate isn't a narcissist?"

BECAUSE MANY A POLITICAL analyst would tell you that it takes a certain amount of narcissism to run for President in the first place. To actually think that you can achieve the highest office in the land, because in the end narcissism equates to self confidence and if you are not confident enough for the job it will tell in the poll numbers, just as Jeb Bush is coming to realize, among other people, lack of confidence and enthusiasm can get you painted, as Donald Trump says, "The Low Energy Candidate."

BUT AS THE hyperbole and hyperness of Donald Trump charges head on with the political power of the Clinton machine, time will only tell who will come out on top. Spectators and commentators are placing their bets, but knowing that their could always be a Trump card, or for that matter a Hillary card that can drastically change the course of events, this is game of chance that this writer is happy to stay out of. Until the last vote is counted on Election Day 2016, it's wise to leave the chips where they lay because there has never been an election that has had the potential to be quite as contentious as the one that lays ahead of us.

Epilogue

SPECIAL SECTION:

Hillary Clinton

8

Hillary's Formative Years

People all over the world know who Hillary Clinton is. Be it as the former first lady, or the strong woman who served as the Secretary of the State, she is surely someone who leaves a strong impression in every single person's memory not only in the USA, but all over the world. Indeed, Hillary Rodham Clinton is not just an ordinary woman who was suddenly thrown into the mixture of men and politics, but someone with a clear view of economics and politics, with her foundation formed from as early as her childhood days.

Born as Hillary Diane Rodham on October 26, 1947, Hillary was then known as the eldest daughter of the couple Hugh Rodham and Dorothy Emma Howell Rodham and a sister to two younger brothers, Hugh Jr. and Anthony. She, along with her two siblings, were raised in Park Ridge, Illinois where her parents owned and managed a rather prosperous fabric store.

Hillary already made herself quite known even as a young child. She was very active in school sports such as baseball, and swimming. She was also an active Girl Scout and Brownie, and had received plenty of awards as one. During high school, she took part in the student council and wrote in the school newspaper. She was able to reach an honorable position at school for her wits, knowledge, and political charisma as part of the National Honor Society in Maine East High School. During her senior year however, she was redirected from East division of their school to the South division; the Maine South High School. Here she showed exemplary performance in terms of academics and was then merited as a National Merit Finalist. She finished high school as one of those who reached the top 5% of their class. Back then, gender is still an issue in USA, but her parents supported her in her choices. Her mother always wanted her to be independent of her choices and make her own name in whatever professional career path she opts to choose. Her father on the other hand, strongly disagrees that gender should be a factor for gaining abilities and opportunities in life.

Hillary was already what you will consider politically aware at such a young age. Her family was politically conservative. She would help canvass South Side Chicago presidential election results. Here, she would spot electoral fraud cases against Richard Nixon who was, at that time, was the Republican presidential candidate.

She attended the Wellesley College for her Bachelor's Degree course, majoring in Political Science, where she became very active in student politics. She became a senior class president in 1969, just before her graduation. She was already hailed as the president of Wellesley Young Republicans even though she was just a freshman. However, her views changed in the later years leading to her stepping down from her position, in which she stated that she considered herself as someone with a mind of a conservative, but with a heart of a liberal. After Wellesley, she attended Yale Law School to have her Master's Degree in Law, where she met Bill Clinton who would be her lover, and later on, as her husband. At some point in her later years, she recalled having been accepted into Harvard for her post graduate studies, but decided to go for Yale instead after being told by a professor in Harvard "we don't need any more women at Harvard" during a student-recruitment party. After graduating from Yale in 1973, she took another course and enrolled at Yale Child Study Center. In here, she took additional courses on medicine and children where she completed one whole year of post graduate course. She focused on child abuse and humbly offered free legal advices to the poor.

Hillary was a Republican in her younger years. She would often participate in young Republican group activities and at one point, campaigned for Barry Goldwater, the Republican Party's presidential nominee back in 1964. However, in 1968, she heard the speech delivered by Reverend Martin Luther King, and she was inspired to work in public service because of this. Since then, she found herself being converted into a Democrat.

She experienced working on several types of jobs while she was studying for college, including her job as a babysitter. At one time, she attempted to apply to NASA but was turned down by the organization, stunning her as she was told that girls cannot participate in the astronaut program. She took an internship at a law firm in Oakland, California which was known for its support of radical causes, constitutional rights, and civil liberties. Bill, whom she was already dating at that time, came and lived with her in California.

In 1971, just after finishing her college Degree, she came to Washington, D.C. and worked for Senator Walter

Mondale. She was assigned to the senator's sub-committee on migrant workers.

Just a year before she finished law school in 1973, she landed a job and actively campaigned for George McGovern, the presidential nominee for Democrats back then. By 1974, just a year after she finishes law school, she was able to become a member of the Presidential impeachment inquiry staff, serving as an adviser to the Judiciary Committee of the House of Representatives back when they were dealing with the Watergate Scandal. After this stunt which resulted to President Richard M. Nixon resigning from his post as President in August, she became a professor at the University of Arkansas Law School. At that time, Bill Clinton, who was her boyfriend and classmate back at Yale Law School, was also a member of the faculty.

9

Hillary as First Lady

As mentioned earlier, Hillary and Bill met in law school, where they were classmates back then.

A few months after she became a member of University of Arkansas' faculty, Bill and Hillary tied the knot on October 11, 1975 and promptly set up their home in Fayetteville. This home was Bill's surprise to Hillary by secretly purchasing it prior to their marriage after the former said she liked the place. They had their one and only daughter five years later, Chelsea Victoria, on the 27th of February in 1980.

A year after their marriage, Hillary continued to work this time, in support for Jimmy Carter's presidency who eventually won the position. Her husband, Bill, was subsequently elected as the Attorney General of the entire country. In 1978, Bill became more active in national politics and won as governor in 1978 in the State of Arkansas at such a tender, young age of 32. He lost his position a couple of years after that in 1980, but was able to quickly redeem himself in the eyes of many by continuously winning in the following elections; 1982, 1984, and 1986.

In 1986, a revision on the US constitution was made stating that the number of years a government official should serve be increased to four from the previous 2 years. In 1990, he once again attempted to run as governor and won. Bill's victory as the governor of Arkansas meant that Hillary, his wife, naturally becomes the city's First Lady. As the city's First Lady, she handled her fair share of governing and public services, including the leadership of the Arkansas Educational Standards Committee, becoming a founder of the Arkansas Advocates for Children and Families, and becoming a board member for the Children's Defense Fund and the Legal Services division of the Arkansas Children's Hospital. In the offside, she became a board member for Wal-Mart and TCBY. By 1988, she was then named by the National Law Journal as one of the most powerful lawyer all over USA; a feat that was yet again repeated in 1991.

By 1992, Bill decided to take his involvement with politics one notch higher by finally entering and running in the presidential campaign. Throughout the years, it was proven how effective and successful she was as a campaign representative and they were able to utilize this with Hillary becoming a valued partner to Bill. At some point during the campaign, Bill would even speak about "twofer" or a presidency where the people would experience having "two presidents for the price of one", pointing out the importance of Hillary not just as a First Lady, but as an important partner especially when it comes to governing the country. This idea was supported by key Democrat figures and Bill eventually won, promptly becoming the President. Bill Clinton then became the President of America with Hillary Clinton by his side as the First Lady of the State.

Hillary kept an active role in the politics in support of

her husband during his reign. Her active participation in the politics eventually drew the ire of the critics however, when she was appointed in the government and set up her own office in the West Wing of the White House. Bill also designated her to become the head of a special Task Force on National Health Reform. The commission was proven controversial when she had all the sessions of her commission closed from the public. However, the commission only lasted for more or less a year, as it was only able to present a complicated Health Reform Plan in the end that was not even considered in either House until the task force was abandoned in September of 1994.

Her hands-on participation in politics received several criticisms. At one time, she fired seven members of the White House travel office staff or the "Travelgate." All her political involvement however, died down as the 1996 election approached, letting her take on a traditional First Lady role.

As First Lady of the State, Hillary was active in promoting reform of the country's Health Care in her capacity as the head of the National Health Reform Committee. Although most of her proposals to provide better health insurance and benefits to the citizens have failed and rejected by the Congress, her efforts proved its worth in raising national consciousness about what was happening with the medical benefits and the problems that the citizens were facing at that time.

Health and human rights are her center of focus in most of her activities during her tenure as the First Lady. She was able to push for the Children's Health Insurance Program, in which the state shall be compelled to provide assistance and support to the children who cannot be supported and provided for by their parents with health coverage. She also provided and initiated a number of programs that would help improve the health of the citizens, including a research funding at the National Institute of Health for the research for illnesses such as childhood asthma and prostate cancer, and assess the illnesses that are affecting the Gulf War veterans, and what assistance they can do to these heroes of war. She also helped with penning and adapting the Foster Care Independence bill, which provides help and assistance to the unadopted children as they transition to adulthood.

One of the duties of the First Lady is to facilitate the conferences and activities in the White House. She held several conferences on children's health and development. She also held conferences about school violence and how to protect the children at school. As a partner to the President, she was known to always have discussions with her husband, and is one of those whom President Clinton would consult before making a particular decision.

Despite her active political role during Bill Clinton's term as a president, she never neglected her duties as a First Lady. She created several programs, including the Save America's Treasures program, which promotes the national effort to provide federal funds and private donations to rescue and help restore iconic historical items and sites from deterioration and destruction. She also initiated the Millennium Project, which provides monthly lectures on America's past and forecasted future. This project was very successful that it paved way for a live simultaneous webcast.

She also took charge in the maintenance and rehabilitation of the White House. She led the restoration of the White House's Blue Room and the redecoration of the Treaty Room. She also spearheaded the creation of the Sculpture Garden in the White House, displaying a large set of contemporary American Works that were loaned from the Jacqueline Kennedy Garden and several other museums. She also hosted several state events, including the St. Patrick's Day reception, state dinners for dignitaries from different countries, and fund raising concerts and events.

What tested Hillary and Bill Clinton's relationship as husband and wife not just in the eyes of people but as political icons of the highest position however, was when the affair of then President Clinton with Monica Lewinsky, an intern in the White House, was brought to public scrutiny. Through it all, from Bill's initial denial to, later on, remorseful admission, Hillary bravely stood by his side. This admission however, prompted a trial that resulted in Bill Clinton being impeached and evicted from his position as the President.

This unfortunate scandal may have ended the reign of Bill Clinton rather tragically. This, however, did not end Hillary Clinton's journey as a famous and strong public figure. This only prompted the beginning of her deeper delve in the world of politics as she finds herself deeper into the complex that would allow her to hold several important positions in the coming years.

10

Hillary the Politician

Just a year after the controversy which prompted the former first family's departure from the highest seat, Hillary made a comeback in the political scene in her own, smart way. The US Senate Seat from New York at that time is about to be vacated by the retiring Daniel Patrick Moynihan who was about to complete his entire four terms of service. With this, Hillary announced her desire to fill in for the position. So that she can legally run as a Senator for New York, she moved out of Washington D.C. and moved to Chappaqua, New York where she, together with the former president, purchased a house to live in. So to speak, her campaign was rather bitter and controversial against the famous Republican Rick Lazio. Surprisingly however, she made history both as the first former First Lady to seek office and at the same time first woman in the history of New York to be elected in the US Senate by winning the election with a rather huge gap of 55% to 43% on her favor. She showed just how well she played her part as a Senator, by actively pushing for health care reform and maintaining her advocacy for the rights and welfare of children.

As a senator, Hillary sat and promptly became a member of four Committees. She was part of the Senate Committee on Armed Services with subcommittee assignments on Emerging Threat and Capabilities, Readiness and Management Support, and Airland; the Senate Special Committee on Aging; the Senate Health, Education, Labor and Pensions Committee holding the subcommittees on Aging, and Children and Families, and the Senate Environment and Public Works Committee with subcommittees on Waste Control, Risk Assessment, Fisheries, Wildlife, Private Property, and Water and Superfund.

In 2001, United States of America suffered the biggest blow that they had ever experienced from the terrorists; the 9/11 attack. This prompted then President George W. Bush's declaration of war against terrorists and attacked Afghanistan. Although Hillary fully supported the attack the government launched, she was critical and had several questions on how the Iraqi War was handled back then. Meanwhile, she was able to secure $21.4 billion in funding to help the State of New York with recovery and clean up. She also provided funds for the Ground Zero redevelopment.

Her efforts to promote health care to the veterans of the war also continued. She maintained her work on the improvement of healthcare benefits of the war veterans. She also sponsored the 21st Century Nanotechnology Research and Development act which aims to provide tax exemption on environmentally conscious construction projects. As part of her commitment to children, she led the funding on creation, renovation, and modernization of public schools. One of the well-appreciated laws that she passed as a Senator was the extension of Unemployment Insurance.

Nevertheless, her support was regarded not only by the government but also by the citizen that in 2007, there were no questions imposed against her credibility as a politician, allowing her to easily bag a reelection without as much as an effort.

In 2008, Hillary believed that she was ripe and ready enough to take on the country as her husband once did. This led to her announcement of her intention to run for president for the Democratic Party. The position was not hers alone, however; as the nomination was also desired by another aspiring candidate; Barrack Obama, the State of Illinois' Senator. She led the polls during the early season of the campaign, but Obama's rather interesting approach and platforms piqued the interest and trust of most Americans that by the 3rd of January, she was only placed as third in the campaign at Iowa. She was able to make a successful rebound during the New Hampshire campaign where she magnificently won the polls, and by the 5th of February, she made a significant lead over Obama for winning over the important states including New York, California, and Massachusetts. The campaign against Obama was rather a close fight, but on June 3rd, Obama successfully became the presumptive Democratic nominee, this becoming official by the 27th of August. Obama's journey to presidency was a success, with him winning and bagging the position as the nation's President on the 4th of November, 2008.

Despite the competition between the two during the campaign for the Democratic Party bid, Obama still see the potential in Hillary and promptly nominated her as the Secretary of State. Hillary accepted the position and was confirmed and appointed by the Senate on January of the following year. Her service as the secretary brought several criticisms due to different controversies she was brought into, but at the same time received several praises for improving USA's relationships with other foreign countries.

As the Secretary of the State, Hillary focused on promoting human and women's rights. She used these as the main points in delivering the country's initiatives to its foreign neighbors and partners. She travelled all over the world; in fact, she was deemed as one of the most travelled secretary in the US history. Halfway through her first term as a Secretary, she already traveled and visited over 77 countries to promote US diplomatic tactics and attend to the concern of the US citizens that are abroad. She also actively promoted using social media as an effective method of conveying to people the positions and plans of USA.

Hillary's main focus as Secretary of the State is to lead and provide international conferences on many different issues about public concern. She heralds and ensures the protection of all US properties and its citizens that are in foreign countries, including diplomat offices and embassies. She also oversees the administration of US immigration laws for US citizens stationed abroad.

She also took a strong stance on US government's behalf when it comes to the country's allies and aggressors alike. She was harshly criticizing North Korea for firing short-range missiles to South Korea, warning them of posing a threat to the peace and stability in Asia. She was also tough on calling out Israel for building establishments and settlements over the disputed areas in Palestine, calling such actions to be insulting. She was known to be a strong supporter on USA's fight against terrorism in Afghanistan, and is active in providing efforts to help reduce terrorism done by Taliban.

As usual, women empowerment and children's rights

are still part of her goals. These may be beyond her duties as a Secretary, but she makes sure to make time for what she considers a lifelong platform and agenda when it comes to serving the public. In most of her international tours, she would often hold "town hall" type of meetings on women empowerment and equal human rights, in which the public will have the opportunity to directly ask her questions on that and other different topics.

On the 11th of September in 2012, USA suffered another deadly attack, particularly on the diplomatic post in Benghazi, Libya where then US Ambassador, Christopher Stevens, and three US diplomat staff were killed. Hillary Clinton, who was then leading the State Department came under scrutiny and investigation over alleged mismanagement and failed security over the US Staff deployed overseas. Hillary, as the leader, took responsibility for this unfortunate happening, prompting her to resign from her post as the Secretary.

Despite her resignation, she is still active in the world of politics and currently released a number of autobiographies of her tales and views in the American Politics.

11

The Issues and Controversies

Getting into several issues and controversies are inevitable in the world of Politics, and Hillary Clinton is not immune to it. From the very start where she dipped her foot into the political arena, she was already showered with several controversies personally, professionally, and politically. These controversies however, may have tested her strength and willpower but this only resulted with her emerging as a strong player in the game, allowing her to gain more support and trust not only from the people around her, but also from her constituents and other key personalities in the foreign field. Two of the biggest scandal and controversies she found herself into are the Lewinsky Scandal in which her husband, Bill Clinton was involved in, and the infamous Benghazi Attack in US's diplomatic office in Libya. These two controversies are very huge in its own definition that it made life-changing decisions in Hillary Clinton's political and private life.

1. *The Lewinsky Scandal*

In 1998, the credibility and strength of the Clinton's relationship as husband and wife was tested at its limit when then President Bill Clinton was embroiled in a controversy involving the 22-year-old White House intern, Monica Lewinsky in an alleged sexual affair. In the local scene, this scandal was called the "Lewinskygate" scandal.

The Lewinsky scandal broke out in 1998 while then President Bill Clinton was serving his second term in the position. Monica Lewinsky, who was 22 years old at that time, was a graduate of Lewis & Clark College and was hired as an intern during Clinton's first term. It was then when their secret relationship happened, as disclosed by her friend Linda Tripp, a worker from the Defense Department who had been secretly recording their telephone conversations whenever Lewinsky confides in her about the relationship.

During the investigation, Lewinsky initially denied the allegations of the said affair. This prompted Tripp to show the tapes to Kenneth Starr, the independent counsel investigating Clinton. Despite the existence of the tapes, Clinton was careful in categorically denying the relationship.

In the end, Lewinsky claimed that there were up to nine different occasions in which she had a sexual encounter with Bill Clinton, seven of those was at the White House with the First Lady Hillary Clinton present and at home. Throughout the accusation, Bill Clinton was insistent on denying the said allegations, contending that he did not sleep nor at any point had a sexual encounter or any relationship with Lewinsky. All throughout, Hillary stood by Bill Clinton's side, protecting and supporting Bill's denial of such claims.

By August of 1998, Clinton finally succumbed to the

accusations and issue, and finally admitted into engaging in an inappropriate relationship with Lewinsky. This prompted a Perjury case against Clinton for lying and for his inappropriate behavior. His license to practice law was also suspended for five years as a result thereof. This admission also prompted an impeachment trial on Bill Clinton. He was, however, acquitted for his perjury case. His improper behavior, however, prompted the Senate to impeach him, forcing him to vacate and leave his office prematurely.

Bill Clinton's credibility to campaign for a Democratic Candidate was also affected. Analysts believed that the scandal that tainted his image would have a lasting effect on the Democratic Party, and that Clinton must be very cautious in endorsing a candidate.

All throughout the controversy, Hillary Clinton dutifully stood by her husband's side, supporting and forgiving. She made sure to let Bill Clinton know that despite his mistakes and shortcomings in life, she is still there to serve as his pillar to support him and his decisions in the future, no matter what.

1. *The 9/11/12 Benghazi Attack*

Another controversy that tested Hillary Clinton's strength as a person not only as a public figure but also as a person with compassion was 14 years later, when the United States experienced a terrible attack in one of its diplomat offices in Libya, more known as the 9/11/12 Benghazi Attack. This rather unfortunate event cost the life of a Diplomat Officer and a few of his staff stationed in Benghazi, Libya, which prompted an investigation from the criticisms the US government received regarding the security of the government employees especially to those that are stationed outside the country. Hillary Clinton, in her capacity as the Secretary of State at that time, claimed responsibility for the unfortunate event that caused the demise of the said government officers in Libya.

On the 11th of September, 2012, the Islamic Militant in Libya attacked the American diplomatic compound, killing then US Foreign Service Information Management Officer Sean Smith, US Ambassador J. Christopher Stevens and two other government staff. The said Islamic riot sprouted from the protests in the country about an anti-Muslim video called "Innocence of Muslims". A captured suspect, Ahmed Abu Khattala, later confirmed that the retaliation was a result of their reaction against the said video. This killing resulted to the people not only in the US but all over the world left with questioning the credibility of the US government to provide proper security to their employees stationed outside the country. After the attack, investigations and trials took place in an effort to point out what went wrong in the security that resulted to such tragic and horrifying end for US Libyan Diplomat Office.

In the later events, al-Qaeda, USA's greatest foe in terrorism, claims responsibility for the attacks that resulted to the death of the government officials. According to a witness, the attack was led by an Islamist militia known as the Ansar al-Sharia in retaliation for the Innocence of Muslims although Ahmed Abu Khattala, the alleged ringleader of the militia, denied taking part in the said attack. Later on, the government observed that a series of attacks on different US government offices took place in the middle east, all of which claims that the said attacks are in retaliation of the anti-Islam movie. President Obama claims that the terrorists and extremists are now just using the said video as an excuse to attack US foreign offices.

A few months after the attack however, Libyan Prime Minister Mustafa Abushagur offered a public apology to the United States and to the whole world. He explains that while they condemn the prejudice against their faith, they likewise strongly condemn using force and terrorism just so to prove their point. He further promised to bring punishment and justice to the people responsible for the said trouble.

On September 13, just 2 days after the said attack, US Libyan Ambassador Ali Aujali offered his personal apology to Hillary Clinton who was the Secretary of the State at that time. He called the unfortunate even a terrorist attack, prompting the warrant for him to issue an apology. He also called the people who died, especially Ambassador Stevens, as a friend and a hero. He also appealed to the US government to continue supporting Libya in spite of what happened.

An investigation was prompted by the Senate following the statement made by President Barack Obama and then Secretary of State Hillary Clinton condemning the incident. President Obama called the attack as outrageous, saying that they will make sure that justice will be done for such unfortunate act of terror. In response to the retaliation, the government also ordered the arrest of the controversial video's producer, Nakoula Basseley Nakoula, and was held in California without bail.

On December, Hillary Clinton was scheduled to appear before the Congress to give her testimony about the Benghazi attack. Five days before the scheduled trial however, Hillary suffered from dehydration and flu and promptly fainted, postponing her impending court appearance. This illness however, was viewed by political rivals such as the Republican Representative Allen West, saying that the alleged illness was intended for Hillary to avoid the trial which was vehemently denied by Clinton's party. The trial was moved to January 23, 2013, where Hillary Clinton was finally able to appear before the congress.

During the trial, Clinton, who was finally giving her testimony on the issue, got into a heated argument with Senator Ron Johnson, who was pressing her for an explanation on why no one from the State Department inquired from the American evacuees if there had been any protests prior to the attack. Clinton, at this point, contends that the issue was the fact that there were Americans who died in Benghazi during the attack, and that the main focus should be to figure out what happened in order to prevent such a thing from happening again and not looking backwards as to why militants decide to attack.

Critics, especially those who are in the Republican Party accused the White House and the State Department for fabricating an inexistent Islamic anger over the movie the "Innocence of Muslim" and constantly pointing to it as the reason for all the events that occurred. By February 2013, Hillary Clinton tendered her resignation as the Secretary of the State, taking responsibility for the entire attack, and taking the blame for the apparent lack of security of the government officials in Benghazi at the time of attack.

Further investigations further point out that the Senior State Department was actually aware of the threat environment in Benghazi, and yet did not act accordingly to provide enough security to the government officials serving in the US diplomat office there.

After her resignation, Hillary took a short break from the political world and instead, opted to serve the people, both Americans and foreigners alike, by taking active participation in the foundation which her husband, Bill formed back in 2001 for humanitarian purposes. She also released a series of books, and took a more active role in promoting Women's Rights and empowerment by engaging in a series of talks and conferences promoting human and women's rights.

www.ingramcontent.com/pod-product-compliance
Lightning Source LLC
Chambersburg PA
CBHW070033040426
42333CB00040B/1670